Reflections of My Soul

Arthur Henn

Angel Publishing
Bradenton, FL

Compiled by Clary Lopez

Publisher:
Angel Publishing
P.O. Box 20044
Bradenton, FL 34204-0004
angelpublishing@verizon.net

ISBN 978-0-6152-0269-3

This book is available at quantity discounts for bulk purchases. For information please contact the publisher

Dedication

I'm dedicating this book of poems to those people who are responsible for my beginnings, first and foremost, God my Lord and savior.

Mom, you are the best mom anyone could have!

Dad, we lost you Fathers Day 2001, I miss you every damn day.

My family, Barbara, Arthur and Aaron, thank you for giving me the space to open my heart to show all "The Reflections Of My Soul"

The rest of you -you know who you are- I love all of you.

Acknowledgments

Clary,

Thank you again for opening your soul to a complete stranger. With out you this book of poems would never have been born.

A book is never the end result of the author's work. The compilation of this book is the foundation of your very hard work. I thank you from the very bottom of my heart.

Debbie,

Thank you, you were the first I asked about writing poems, in so many words to keep it short you told me to listen to my heart and write about my emotions, things going on around me and you told me that I would find my voice. I have found my voice and that voice is my soul. Thank You.

Foreword

My soul is that hidden voice that no one sees or really knows. I hear it speak to me everyday. These poems are the hidden words, emotions, feelings, and a way of thinking, rooted deep inside this soul of mine.

A song, a sunrise, a sunset, the beauty of a beautiful woman set in the path of my eyes, inspiration that will birth a poem. This is where my poems come from.

Life and its surroundings, my truest feelings, thoughts weaved from letters to words to a poem from what my eyes see, *"Reflections of My Soul."* What one sees on the out side is rubbish, what you read through my poems is the real me.

Clary, you are the binder of my soul.

Debbie, you are the cornerstone of each word I write.

To all the rest, you know who you are. I love all of you! Thank you for making me smile.

Reflections of My Soul

Soul Searching

Breaking down the barriers
Fighting what's inside me
Life and all its changes
Overwhelmed
Longing for your soul
~
In the silence of my heart
What does one seek?
Love, Truth, or Dare
The path I question
Locked up at night
In the darkness of my soul
~
Who I was, who I am
Who I want to be
~
This soul of mine
Is a missing person
Wanting to crawl back
Inside of me
~
Exposing my truest feelings
On paper for all to see
My mind is a cable
Running from my heart
To my soul
~
Your eyes see
Only what your mind reads
My heart is the center
Of what I believe
~
Looking for love
That never was there
My heart is in love
With your beautiful soul

This Is Who I Am

I see evil, evil in your eyes
There have been many days of my life
Silence has surrounded me
Unforgiving wanting to fight
Fighting evil, rising in me
~
My heart shines
Shines upon you
With its reflection
Of love
Evading solitude within my heart
~
The beast lies dormant
Covered with true love
True love that comes from deep down
Deep down in the pit of my soul
Waking up
Showing emotions of
Who I really am
~
This is who I am
Showing you
Reflections of my soul

This Heart

I live in
Homage to my soul
Stucco and grayed
...
Her eyes hold the keys
To my soul
...
Her fragrance
Flows steadily through out the night
Playful and soft
...
Creeping through the cracks in the floor
Hearing her voice calling
...
Sweet rain
Whispering
Melodies in my ear
...
Tears running down my cheeks
Missing her sweet embrace
Longing for yester years
...
Weathered and wasted
Another bottle of wine
Just to ease the pain of loneliness
I see her smile
Feeling her embrace
...
Down and out
Not knowing what to do
I see her loving arms reaching down from heaven
I smile, remembering
Times shared
Shared by hearts embraced
Embracing troubled waters
...
Our lives are just a memory
A memory
Of love and joy

To love you

Is to die for you
To die for you
Is
To love you
~
Your beauty escalades
Beyond measure
~
You are the sunrise
Embracing darkness
You are God's painted sky
The reflection
Of
What's in the iris
Of
His eyes
~
Peacefulness surrounds you
His loving arms
Embrace you
Let him guide you
~
Guide you to the center of the storms

Take My Hand

My mind
Is in your time capsule
Wanting time to stand still
Lets make this moment last
Lets
Let it grow
~
Through out our universe
When I look into
The depth of your eyes
I see your garden grow
~
Each rose
Is out of reach
I see richness of color grow
I smell the fragrance of your soul
~
Walking every mile
Of your rose garden
That grows
My mind
No longer a capsule
Its reality
Standing here
Wanting
To make love
To you

Teased

With the pleasure of spirits
Fresh fruit flavored Merlot
Inhaled with every sip
Awakens new words
Unearthed in my soul
I write these words

~

How many times have I looked into your eyes?
Telling you I love you
Telling you I need you

~

I'm so lonely
It's not any surprise
I'm missing you
Day and night

~

Telling you I love you
Is more important than the air I breathe
What more can I say

~

The Merlot I drank tonight
Has my soul satisfied
Saying things I want
But shouldn't

~

Why am I saying these things?
One does not know

The Beauty of Mother Nature

Illuminates all
In her power
With the warmth of a morning kiss
~
She's enchanting
She's electrifying
She's
"Mother Nature"
At
Her best
~
Her winds
Change
Changing at will
~
She lights up her skies
Like
Fire flies
Dancing in the night
~
Calm and cool
She sways with her moods
~
Seductive
Looking for one to kiss
Embracing your cheek with a warm kiss
~
She warms up the nights
With
A summer night's breeze
~
Shades of color
Unfolding
With each morning sunrise
~
Gods sedating skies
Putting her darkness
To rest
~

What surprise
Will she have for us next?
~
Beautiful as she is
She can be a torrent
At times
Angry and wicked
Letting us know
She's everything
But
"Mother Nature"
At
Her best
~
Yes
She has a temper too!
~
She bows her head
Eyes
Looking upon her creator
Asking for forgiveness
~
No longer angry
Only beautiful

"Mother Nature"
At her best

The Souls of 911

The two of us
Standing tall
Embracing one another's
Love
~
The livelihood
Of
Our inner
Souls
~
Running with the security
Of living souls
~
This day
Blue skies
Reflect
What's in our souls
~
Peering out
The darkness of my soul
I see pain fall up on you
Sadness fills my soul
Not understanding
Why they took you away
From me
~
Standing tall
Alone
I feel insecure
Missing you
Watching
You fade away
~
Watching
What took you down
Coming my way
~
My arms, now gone
For you took them with you

Arthur Henn

~
Unable to fight back
My soul crumbles
Into smoke and fire
~
Loved ones
Running through
The city streets
Tears running down their
Hearts
Searching for the ones they love
~
Lying here with you
Finding my arms
That use to hold you
I embrace you one last time

This Heart of Mine

Love in all its power
Admiration for one another
Two hearts fill each other
By means of kindness and joy
~
Love for each other
Forever a burning desire
Close your eyes
Say a prayer
Turn a page
True love will be there
~
A prayer answered
God knows your journey
Your friendship, act of kindness
Is here to stay
~
You need time alone
This heart will always have
Room for you
You are hurting, he's not
This heart of mine
Wants to embrace
Your sorrow
~
Say a prayer
Turn a page
You have just
Found true friendship
Standing here
~
Two hearts joined together
For the love and admiration
For one another
By means of kindness and joy
~
Never look back
Keep moving forward

Arthur Henn

Thank God for answered
Prayers

Missing You

I sit on this empty bed
We made love in
Watching you gracefully move across the room
~
Our souls still dance with each other
When you sleep
~
Watching you sleep
Always brings a smile to my face
This is the only time you smile
~
Every time you close your eyes
Your dream becomes a reality
I caress the softness
Of your inner soul
You feel the softness
Of a sweet embracing kiss
Tender kiss
On your lips
I whisper in your ear
"I Love You"
~
You roll over
Hugging your pillow
Waking up, looking into
Another early morning sunrise
~
What was reality
Was just another dream
~
You stand looking out towards the rose garden
We walked through every morning
I stand here beside you
Whispering in your ear
Standing In front of the window pane
Watching the reflection of me embrace you
~

Missing me
You don't
Know I'm here
~
My soul, wanting you to see me, the way I see you,
You wouldn't be so lonely
~
My hand reaches out for yours
As you caress the softness of your breast
The way I use to
~
A shiver runs up and down your spine
As if you felt another in the room
You smile, looking upon the empty bed
Tears run down your cheeks
It's only a memory
~
You sense
I'm on the other side
Of the door
Your desire to open it causes you to look
~
We make eye contact
You walk right through me
As if I'm not there
~
Your mind is made up
You're going to have a good time
Staying out with the girls tonight
But you can't stop thinking of us
~
Baby
Were just memories
Please let lose of me
~
Your emotions overwhelm you
You feel the presence of me
Running back to your room
Your soul feels a desire
To look out the window pane

Reflections of My Soul

~

Running your hand across the glass
You feel my fingertips pressing into yours

~

You see the reflection of me holding you
You turn around
I'm not there

~

If only we could hold each other
One more time

~

We could make a memory

Unable To Be Tamed

By winds of change
I follow you through storm clouds
Serenading you with winds of
"Mother Nature"
Rain mixed with tears
Tears of sorrow, turned into
Joy
~
Letters of words caught in my web
Feelings of emotions,
Turned into words
~
Fastened by love of another
Secret recesses,
Flow through my fingertips
Feelings of melodies
Wander throughout the night
Embraced, framed by this poem
Through a poem
Embracing the love for one another,
Turning into
True friendship
Friendship that will last
Forever!

Veil of Secrecy

Your veil of secrecy
Inhibits revolving doors
~
Mysteries of your mind
Disguised in enveloped smiles
Why do you keep your beauty hidden?
In un-expressed ways
~
Your smile
Your invisible smile
Shines through the iris of your eyes
~
Lifting your veil of secrecy
I embrace your lips with a tender kiss
A kiss that opens
Opens up doors
Doors no longer revolving
But standing still
~
Your soul, now open
Standing open
Growing with love
Love to share
~
I want to know everything there is about you
What you do when I'm not there
What you think about
When you look at yourself
In the mirror
~
Memories wishing I was there
With you
~
I lie here wondering what it would be like
Loving you
All through the night
~
We can make this night a journey
A journey to remember

Arthur Henn

January through December
~
Let's make love
Let's uncover the veil of secrecy
For eternity

We Sail Together

On a moon that rises in the blackness of night
No where to go
Falling stars shine in your eyes
Your beautiful eyes, reflect the image
Of this nights moon
Moonbeams rest on your shoulders
Your shoulders naked to the night
~
Night moves
In harmony of your thoughts
Running my hands through your soft hair
I stroke your lips
Embracing them with a soft kiss
~
You smile
Your eyes, light up the darkness
Of my soul
The warmth of your soul
Embraces my heart
On this oceans breeze
We sail together
No one knows
The journey of our souls

What a Dream It Was

Only the beginning
I remember it all started with a kiss
On the back of her knee
she murmurs words in French
I don't understand
~
I can still taste and feel her soft lips
looking into her eyes
Remembering her smile
the mole that landscaped
The top corner of her lip
a beauty mark
The signature of her soul
~
I cradle her lovely face
In the palm of my hands
caressing her lips with mine
I wake up only to realize
it's a dream
~
What a dream it was
I still smell her perfume
And taste her lips
this is only the beginning
of another dream

What If

Let your soul be your guidance
Let my tears meet up with yours
Lost inside of you
You are a blessing from above
I Love You

~

Never lose faith in me
I will always be your truest friend
I won't walk away
My soul is connected to yours
You say you are lonely
Its time to let him go
Your life is too precious
To hurt evermore
Your soul is loved by another

~

Please forgive me
If my words seem harsh
Knowing you deserve better
Wishing I could fill his shoes

~

Let's dance, let's dance the night away
Dancing your sorrows away
Bringing a smile to your beautiful face
Gracefully holding you, swaying across the floor
We stop; I look into your eyes
Seeing the reflection of Gods painted sky

~

I wonder
What if
Realizing
You do deserve better
Letting your soul be you guidance
Not wanting you to hurt anymore
I shed a tear for you

What Will We Leave Behind

This morning's sunrise
Unfolds light upon this nights darkness
~
Winter storm clouds fade away
~
The birth of spring
Brings on death of winter
She takes her last breath
Mother Nature gasps for air
God closes her windows
Opening her doors
~
She renews her last breath
With that of spring
~
Everything that lives
Has
A cycle
~
In the cycle of life,
Death will surely come
Renewed by life's
Full circle
~
The birth of
Spring
The beginning of Mother Natures
First season
God's majestic colors
Unfold for our eyes to see
~
Her colors, fragrance in the air
~
A baby bird is born
She chirps among the young
A mother cries pains of joy
Laboring birth into a new season
Of joy
Like that of a baby bird chirping

Reflections of My Soul

This baby will cry
~
At death we die
At birth we cry
The death of one
The birth of another
Life begins
A new cycle
~
Spring begins a new cycle
A new breath becomes the sister of our souls
Our souls become
The greatest gift of all
Faith of the one living in us
The mysteries of life unfold upon us
~
The suns rays blanket the earth's soil
With warmth
The mysteries of nature unfolds
~
How can not one believe?
There's a beginning
There's an ending
What will we leave behind?
Are we just memories for someone else to share?

With Out Each Other

I felt the rain
Fall between our lips
~
Your soul caressing mine
~
What are we
With out each other
~
Separated by time
~
Time is of essence
Like the first spring rose
~
It's beauty for all to admire
For all to see
~
A scent unequal
To that of a woman
~
I Cherish
Your beautiful soul

Your Beautiful Mind

Is the sunset
God used
To put my mind to rest
~
Your beautiful mind
Was the sunrise
I looked into
Thinking of you
~
Your friendship
Continues to grow
Like a summer rain
~
It's the greatest part
Of whom you are
~
You are one of a few
Yes
The very first one
That stood out from the rest
~
Beauty to be admired
Letters from your heart
Turned into words
Molded into a beautiful
Poem
~
A poem for all to read
Cherish
For the rest of their lives
~
Like the first rose of spring
Rain delicately running off your petals
A memory set in my mind
Your bouquet
Never
Never leaving
But resting
In between the words

Arthur Henn

That escapes your beautiful
Mind

Random Thoughts

This night I look to the west
The rays of the sun descends
As if into some soft substance
Or place creating a painted sky
~
A crescent moon shines above the horizon
Like a curved thumb nail in the night sky
The colors of darkness
Are not present this night
What will become of such a night?
~
The winds of change gust through the valleys
The sky is clear this cold dark night
Upon my morning, I look to the east
The rays of the sunrise
Creating a painted sky
The crescent shaped moon, still clear
As it was last night
~
Colors of daylight budding
Yellow to orange, expanding to deep dark blue
Space blue
Silhouetted mountains
Silhouetted palm trees
Hugged by this graceful mood
~
Morning star shines bright
All is calm
Surreal, beautiful, brisk and cold
My mind is open not knowing what to write
Caffeine flowing through my veins
The thought of life's torments subdue my mind
The struggles I face in life
The struggles we all face in life
~
Wanting to write poetry, the center of my soul
Only to break away from reality
What does one do, while the other sleeps
~

My thoughts are still only random thoughts
I think of this world as a world gone mad
Time continues to move
There's no stopping time
She awakens; it's six am
She smiles, saying thank you for last night
~
Smiling, thinking to myself, what did I do right?
My thoughts are still only random thoughts
Her lips, the curve that runs down her back
The seam that runs down the back of her
stockings
Stirs my imagination
My thoughts are still only random thoughts
~
What will become of our nation?
What are these words I write?
Where do they come from?
Life is full of surprises
One does not know, what direction to go
East, west, south or north
~
The sound of broken glass, falling on the floor
My mind wanders with many thoughts
Trying to think of what to write
These are words of random thoughts
~
My mind is restless
Thoughts of anger
Thoughts of joy
Thoughts of passion
Thoughts of when she last looked into my eyes
The smell of her perfume
Is life real, or is it just a random dream
One day when I reawake, what will I see?
~
What we see in front of us
Is it really what we see?
~
A tree, a bird, a rose
The sunrise, the sunset

Reflections of My Soul

Is it really everything were told it is?

~

The world is a culture of different skin color
Were all just one race
What's the big deal about world culture?

~

Why does man separate himself?
Out of his race, the color of another mans skin
The love for one another should be like
A glove of warmth on our hands
These are just random thoughts

Reflections

Looking outside this window
Seeing life pass in front of me
I see hatred
I see love
When is it all going to change?
~
It's late at night, I'm driving on the wrong side of
the road
She's resting up against my shoulder,
Earlier this night she was standing on a street
corner
Nowhere to go!
~
Music playing on this old radio
I think were somewhere in the middle of Texas
Snow starting to fall, she snuggles up close, to be
warm
Reaching over to cover her, with my jacket
Not expecting it to snow
I think to myself
Why does a love between two have to end on a
street corner
In the middle of Texas
~
She wakens to a bump in the road
Tired, having a hard time keeping on my side of
this old road
Pulling into the parking lot of an old diner
Neon light buzzing
"Open 24 hours"
Looking up at me she smiles
"Are you hungry?"
I ask
"Just hold me"
She responds
~
I put my arm around her, kissing her on the
forehead

Reflections of My Soul

I cradle hear tearful expression in the palm of my
hands
Wiping tears from her cheeks with my thumbs
I tell her
"Let's go get some coffee"
~
She looks at me, I look at her
I see a desire of emotion running through her
soul
Lord help me make it through this night, for I
know her thoughts
She has been through enough, she doesn't need
me
Again looking into her eyes
Tears start to flow
~
"You ok"
I ask her
~
"Lie with me tonight"
She responds
Words softly spoken
My heart races, she doesn't know what she's
asking
My heart aches, wanting to comfort her soul
~
Wait here; I'll be right back
Running across this old parking lot, I get a key
for a room
Both of us walking up the stairs
I unlock the door; I cradle her smiling face,
telling her goodnight
"Won't you come lie with me tonight"
she responds
~
Words softly spoken
"This warm bed is just for you"
I'll be right here in this old truck
"Sweet dreams goodnight"

Restoring One's Faith

In the depth of our souls,
No one understands the perception
Of our faith, of what we believe
~
Looking deep within the darkness
Of our souls
Demons sleep, put away forever
But the beast still exists
~
Deceived, the mirror of existence
Afraid to step forward, into the light,
Of existence
~
Why are we afraid?
God knows all,
What we don't see, he sees
~
Growth from within ones soul
Grain against grain,
The walls of all
God's glory
~
Callused souls, no longer rough, but smooth
Looking into the light
Cultivating, Refining, Cleansing, Polishing,
Purifying,
Focusing, making purer,
Restoring ones faith
~
Resurfacing, repairing a broken heart
Repairing all our broken hearts, so we can love
again!

Romance under a Moonlit Sky

Romance shared by two hearts
Passion moves through out the night
Under a moon lit sky
~
Her eyes
Dark as the night sky
Mirror images of this night
Full moon
Lights up beauty while I look
Into her eyes
~
Wanting to embrace her
Trying to hold back
Emotions that encircles my heart
A spark of desire
Troubled she will turn away
~
Asking her
May I hold you?
Upon these hours of darkness
~
We dance swaying back and forth
Under the moonlight
I kiss her behind the ear
She shudders
Embracing me, unyielding
~
Her hair, her skin
Soft as silk,
My senses scent her perfume
The aroma of rose petals
Blanket the lawn
For us to lie down on
~
My heart opens up to her
She walks in
Feeling each others
Warmth of joy

She's a Woman

She cries
She loves
She hides her emotions
She's your companion
She's your woman
Treat her like one

~

She's a lady
She's graceful
In every way she moves
The way she carries herself
Like wild flowers swaying
In the sunlit fields
Vibrant with color
If not nourished with warmth
She will diminish in color

~

They cry
They love us
They show their emotions
They're our companions
They're our women
Let's treat them delicately
Let's nourish their souls
Hungry for love
They will let us know
When they want to be
Loved

Reflections of My Love

Looking beyond the arch of love
I watch her dance, gracefully swaying
Across the floor
Wishing these arms of mine
Were the ones holding her
~
The reflection of my love
Ripples across the fountain water
Sending melodies into the air
Hoping they touch her soul
~
We make eye contact
She smiles
My heart stops
Reaching out to her
Asking for her hand
May I have this dance?
~
Skies that were gray
Are now blue,
With Gods painted sky
Turning from dusk
To a cloud covered full moon
~
I whisper into your ear
I love you
Caressing you
Through out the early morning hours
~
This morning sunrise erupts
As I
Look upon its colors
In the iris of you beautiful
Blue eyes

She Smiles Again

Around here these ships guide their way
Through her storm channel
~
The setting sun
Sets in her narrow abyss
This evening's painted sky
Reflects off rocks piled high
Around her
~
She sits looking for the one she loves
The beckon that shines across the way
Lights up her beauty every day
Casting shadows across her landscape
She lights up the sky like thunder
~
When God looks into her eyes
A magical mystery that glows in her eyes
Seen by every ship that passes by
~
I look upon her through this telescope
The colors of her soul
An exhibition
Beauty and emotions
Set in a bracelet of charms
Encircling her wrists
With love
Waiting for the one she loves
~
She dances in mother natures winds
Showing her soul
Smooth as pearls
Eyes darker than olives
During the day
~
Her mole, the beauty mark of her soul
True feelings here to come
Wishing she would stay
Not forgetting
She holds me in the palm

Of her hands
~
Guided by her gentle care
Having no fear
Of what's in front of me
She sleeps
Dreaming of the next sunrise
Holding me in the palm of her hands
~
I lie with her in the midst of her dream
Her mind is in perfect harmony
The emotions that grow beneath her soul
She becomes weary
Storm clouds work their way around her
Her long brown hair
Delicately blows in this stormy weather
As it lays back down
Along her back
~
She turns her beautiful face
Resting on her shoulder
Embracing for the worst
She's a delight to look upon as I watch her
In this beckons flashing light
Fog whistles blow in the distance
She awakens
I see her movement
Upon her pile of rocks
She looks down on me
She smiles again
Like she has so many times before
~
There's something about her
That keeps me coming back
I'm the one she's been waiting for
A dream
No longer a dream
But reality
~
The storm's calm
Every time our eyes meet

Arthur Henn

The fog vanishes
The whistles stop blowing
Her true beauty
Shows once more
Her fragrance makes its way down
To my ship
I wonder if she's real

She's not like the Rest

Watching her from a distance
She stands on a street corner
Day and night
Her hair gently flows in the wind
Why is she here
Who will she sleep with tonight?
~
Her legs
Those heels
The seams that run up and down her stockings
Graceful as she is
You wouldn't know
She was a lady of the night
~
I pass her by on the street
She smiles
I smile back
My heart races
My mind wonders
What is a beautiful woman like this?
Doing on the streets at night
~
She dresses like no ordinary woman
She's a class act
I stop
Turning around for one last look
A typical thing for a man to do
She looks back
Stops and smiles
Standing in front of a Starbucks Café
I ask her if I could buy her a cup of coffee
~
Why are you doing this?
I ask
She said I didn't need her in my life anymore
Who would have known
We'd be sitting
Across

From each other
Drinking coffee
~
Hearts on fire
Empty space between our souls
Justified
Balanced
Wanting to testify our love for each other
She cries
Kissing her tears away
I take her hand
Walking under the midnight stars
Loving each other in a special way
Growing inside her
Passion overwhelms my soul
I'm in this old pick-up
Driving to work
She know longer stands on the street corner
I shake my head
Telling myself
It's only a dream

Murky Wells

I sit here waiting
In the blackness of space
On the other side
Of midnight
~
Darkness, creeping in through
Our eyes
The pain we feel
In each others
Hearts
Yes these wells are deep
Deep with hopes
Hopes that one
That one so called God
Can reach down
Pull us up
Out of this murky well
~
We look up
Seeing the reflection of
Light shining off the water
We hear running down the side
Of this well were in
~
A well so deep
With frustration
If we all really knew
What God knows
Why won't he tell us?
His
"Secret"
Secret to those that really wants help
Help in ways
Knowing we have reached a dead end

Mom

She lives her days being a mother
Devoted, watching her little ones grow
Nine months, hidden from this outside world
Nourished by Gods magical life line
Sheltered
Protected by her womb
~
Feeling movement
She smiles
Knowing life resides
In that special place
Growing, knowing all is well
~
The gift of life
Born, separated
Bonded, nourished by your bosom
The heart of your soul
~
Weaned to be fed by a spoon
Unaccustomed to surroundings of love
The bridge of life
Separates the two of you
~
First steps are taken
Reaching out to you
Falling into your loving arms
Having faith
Faith with laughter, a smile
Knowing you will be there
~
Separating themselves
Departing to the outside world
Sympathetic, supporting
Their walk in life
Carefully weaning yourself
With gentle tender love
~
Embraced

Reflections of My Soul

By the love of another
Your gifts walk in your footprints
Unable to fill them
~
Shining back upon you
They smile
With open arms
"Thank You"
"Mom"

Missing Me Tonight

I wonder what clothes you wear
I wonder what you see
When you look into your mirror
At night
~
I'm standing here behind you
You cannot see me
But you can feel me
You disrobe your beautiful
Gown you wore tonight
~
You went to a party
Dressed all in white
Everyone there
Including myself
Thought you looked wonderful tonight
~
You turn out the light
Thinking of what's right
Staring upon my photo
That hangs on the wall
Missing me tonight

Majestic Color

Mother Natures
Beauty
~
Not only can I feel
The quietness of her soul
My eyes
Embrace
The
Stillness
Of
Her early morning sunrise
~
Her majestic entry
Just before she opens her door
~
In admiration
Of her beauty
The way
I feel
Her arms
Unfold
Upon me
~
She warms
My soul with tenderness
And
Amusement
~
The smile
She brings
Upon my appearance
~
My compassion
Longs
For her to stay
Right here
Where
She
Lays

~
Relaxed
As I am
~
In seclusion
Within her perfection
Not wanting to let
Her
Go

Lovers of the night

Holding hands
Walking up and down the beach
Waves roaring upon their feet
Under this nights moonlit sky
~
God's creation of beauty
Unfolds over them
Stars diminishing into the open sea
Sand crystals, etched,
Between their toes
~
Their souls dance
Amongst the midnight air
Lying down in the sand
Feeling the left over warmth
God planted in the sand
~
Looking into her sea green eyes
He sees reflections of Gods falling stars
Softly kissing her lips
He makes a wish
~
Wishing she wouldn't fade away
Amongst the emerald green sea
Hiding with the stars, like she has
So many times before

Love That Reigns Forever

The night is still
The moons rays of light
Shine out from behind her
Silhouetting her long beautiful
Blond hair
~
She rides through this mystical garden
A rose garden
Nurtured from the heavens above
On a white mare
~
Looking for the one she loves
The night is still
The moons rays of light
Shines upon him
Shining bright off his armor
Reflecting soft sparkling light
Into her eyes
~
Pulling up hard on the reigns
Of the stallion he rides
Both horse and riders
Rise to a stand off
Of the unknown
~
Battle torn tides of emotions
Reign over their hearts
Looking into each others eyes
For the first time
Stallion and mare
Standing side by side
~
He Bowes
She Bowes in shame of her mare
He takes her hand lightly kissing it
Looking upon her
Her head still bowed
Showing emotions of interest
~

This rose garden shining under this moon lit sky
Romance blooms amongst the heavenly stars
Their eyes sparkle amongst the beauty of each
rose
The fragrance of rose bushes blooming at their
feet
~
This reign of love
Turns two souls that love each other
Into matrimony
~
Two burning candles
Lit
To light one
To show the universe
Their love for each other
~
Smiles grow upon their faces
As they embrace each other
Loving one another as one
~
Growing inside her
Soft moans flow through out this night
As they give up each others gift to one another
Growing old together
Living a faithful life together as king and queen
~
One dies
She places him in a tomb
A cold wind blows through
Where he lies
~
What once was the garden of love
Is now the garden of death
These roses have not bloomed since
Her loves death
~
Leaves scurry across this cold wind blown ground
Storm clouds
Light up this night's dark sky
Rain falls

Arthur Henn

Mixing with tears
Running down her cheeks
The cold wind brushes them away
Looking upon his tomb
She remembers the true
Faithful love
They shared

Love struck

On a Sunday afternoon
Setting, watching her
From afar
Her gracefulness fixed my eye
Predetermined life's story
~
Heels, ankle length dress
Dressed in white cotton
In awe of her beauty
I smile
~
Looking out towards the waterfront
Both our souls embrace
Each other
Walking shorelines
~
Unable to control my emotions
I ask for her hand
~
We walk life's secret garden
~
We dance
~
Melodies of happiness
Flow throughout the course of the night
~
Looking into her eyes
Holding her face
Stroking her hair
Kissing her temples
Rubbing her neck and shoulders
I whisper in her ear
You're an angel
Embraced by her fragrance
~
Barley brushing lips together
We kiss
Telling each other goodnight

Love Mixed With Passion

The lights are turned down low
Candlelight dancing off the walls
White string pearls
Draped around you beautiful neck
~
Secret garden fragrances
Flowing through the air
Rose petal trails
Line the path of love
~
Love mixed with passion
Signs of emotions
Our smiles overwhelms
The moon, that rises
Looking into your eyes
Watching
The other side of midnight
Embrace
The mere early morning hour
~
Take my hand,
Let's walk through
Your Secret garden
The one that adorns your soul
Through eternity

Love, Peace, Comfort and Joy

These love filled words
That I have not spoken
You my dear, dream dreams
Of this love summer filled afternoon
~
You awaken, embraced
By this mornings early sunrise
You hurdle, life's hurdles
One after another
~
You close your eyes
With a prayer in mind
Praying for love, Peace,
Comfort and Joy!
~
God embraces your beautiful soul
Lifting you up
You endure life's strongholds
Giving up yourself,
For the comfort of others
~
Your sun shines once more
Setting with the dove
The white dove's of Love, Peace,
Comfort and Joy!
~
Your summer filled dreams,
Of Love, Peace, Comfort and Joy!
Becomes God's reality

That Which Was Written In Stone

Love that once was,
Has settled like dust
Deceived of ones own hatred by another mans
belief
We seal in faith
~
That which was written in stone
One does not believe,
Stories that were once told
Mans mind brews storms
~
Times of love, passion
Are no more
The sun will set and rise on another mans plea
~
Essence of both men's plea
Long overdue
Deceived of his own hatred
Hatred that shouldn't be
~
Men, woman and children
Slumber off into dreams
Dreams that unfolds
Into the emptiness of ones mind
Valleys of love

Passion Runs Wild

She dances in the middle of the night
Dreaming
Dreaming of the one she loves
Hearts of fire
Encircle her un-rested
Soul
~
Waterfalls cascading behind her
She feels the mist rising up off Her Soothing,
weary soul
~
Floral fragrance embraces
Her beautiful hair
Graceful as she is
She thinks she has to dance
Dancing the night away
~
She's sensual
In every way she moves
Passion runs wild through her soul
Fashion at its best
Worn by this beautiful soul

Not Giving Up

Boxed in by six panes
Of un-broken glass
Glass I will not let break
Pain and discomfort
No one else feels
Wanting what's best
For us all
~
Why does it rain?
When there's
Not even a cloud in the sky
~
Crossroads
Beyond every block
I stand in the middle
Of each one
Not knowing which corner
To hug
~
Can't make up my mind
Which path to follow
Wanting to give up
I won't
For who knows what tomorrow
Brings

Never Out Of Reach

Thoughts of you unfold in my mind
Your beauty surpasses all imagery
Of what you would look like
~
A song dear to my heart
Wild horses
I hear you sing over and over
Your voice
Your sweet harmonic voice
Imposes the beauty of your soul
The soul my body has been searching for
~
When our bodies sleep
Our souls meet
Dancing to the sweet melodies
Of your mind
~
We listen to music
Reminding each other
Were never out of reach
~
Never will we depart
We are not that far apart
For the rest of my life
I will always think of you
All I want to say
Is
I Love You!

Needing You

Holding your face
Your beautiful face
Gazing Into Your Eyes
You look amazing

~

Stroking your hair
Kissing your temples
Rubbing your neck and shoulders
Our souls dance the night away

~

Softly I touch
Long gentle caresses
Barley brushing our lips together
My eyes look deep into yours

~

Embracing your warm smile
I kiss you passionately
The warmth of your soul
Embraces mine

~

We dance the night away

~

Under the moonlit sky

Nature Comes To Pass

They both position themselves
Along side one another
Together creating sounds of passion
Nature comes to pass
~
Arrives, as in due course
To life's magical mysteries
Gods painted ski descends
As if into some soft substance
Penetrating its great abyss
~
Darkness settles in
Her crescent formed companion rises
Above his morning glory
Winter falls
Spring rises
Nature subdues
To the warm embrace
Of our suns passionate
Kiss
~
She smiles
He smiles
Embracing each other
With open arms

Never Looking Back

The look in your eyes tells a story
Someone you love has drifted away
Tears falling down your cheeks
Nowhere to go
~
The sun rises this morning
Encompassing
A path for you to go
A path of love that follows
Close behind
You
~
Never looking back
You keep moving forward
Forward into paradise
A paradise of love
That know one has found
~
The fragrance you smell
Like no other
Has been waiting for you
~
Its heart shaped
Rose garden
A paradise
That will
Love
You

My Love is Pure

My heart yearns for your soul
Every time we walk the paths
Of your garden
After midnight,
Lit up by this nights
Full moon
~
Another place, another time
What shall we do?
I'm so caught up in you
~
The Desire, The Passion, Running towards you
Wanting to embrace you
Loving You
Throughout, the early morning hours
~
The break of day
Softly glows on your bare shoulders
The sun sets
The moon rises
All in one day
~
This soul of mine is pure
My eyes light up
When I kiss you
I want to tell the world
How much
"I Love You"

My Heart is an Open Gate

~

With this heart of mine
These open arms
Want to hold you

~

My heart won't stop
Longing for you

~

The pain
The sorrow
The loneliness
That holds you tight

~

My heart is an open gate

~

Walk in
Sit down
Let me ease your pain
Let me ease your sorrow
Let me fill your loneliness

~

I know these are dark days
Turn your back
Towards the storm

~

Look into my eyes

~

Let me kiss
Your tears away

~

I will shelter you
With my soul

~

My soul is reaching
Out to you

~

Taking your hands
I turn you around

Reflections of My Soul

Holding you close
Cradled in my arms
~
We both sway to melodies
From your heart
~
Looking into
Gods painted sky
Seeing the storm
Depart
Opening the gates
Of heaven
He smiles
~
You feel his warmth
Embrace your heart
~
Not wanting to let go
Of these arms
Holding you

Arthur Henn

My Arms Are Open to You

Captivated
By her beauty
Watching her

~

Her woman hood
The most delicate
Flower
I comfort myself in

~

The way she moves
Gracefully moves
Amongst
The other swaying
Flowers

~

Her secret garden
Rooted in the soul
Of her heart

~

Nourished
By the warmth
Of the rising
Sun

~

She's in reach
Of new growth
Growth
Renewing her soul

~

The soil
She looks down on
Withered and cold

~

Lonely
She is

~

Wanting

~

Someone

To be there
For her

~

Someone
To just listen
While she speaks

~

Someone
With open arms
To just hold her

~

Someone
To love her
When she's
Ready

In my life

There has been solitude
And
Gratitude
~
Never having a girl in my life
As beautiful as you
~
You are poetry in motion
Letters molding themselves into words
Words moving with desire
Desire running with passion
To show how much
~
I Love You
~
Your love leans towards every corridor
~
Your look
Is a look
Of
Desire
~
If you need somebody,
I'm standing
Right here beside
You
~
Do you want me?
The way
I want you
~
I want you like the sunrise embracing
Darkness
~
Your eyes stand out
With the soft colors of a butterfly
~

Skin, soft as lamb's wool
Nothing more beautiful
Than the other side
Of
Midnight

Is This Not Real

~

The invisible world of emotions
Whose hearts will they touch?
Words on a screen
So close to that of reality
We feel
We touch
We smell
We sense
Emotions of one another
Is this not real?

~

Is it just the dream of fingertips
Pressing keys on a key board
Turning our feelings
Into emotions
For another to see

~

I wonder
Why do some stay?
Why do some leave?
Why do I get so emotionally involved?

~

The mind is a magical garden
A garden of what ever you want your eyes to see

~

So what is it about this invisible world?
Of emotions
Do we really exist?
Or is it just, make believe
Of what we want our hearts to see

Journal of Love

Tender is the night, not wanting to let you go
The times we sat out in the middle of the lake
Thinking everyone forgot us
But
"Mother Nature"
~
The times we shared space, in each others minds
Swept off our feet, taken to the highest high
Holding each other, loving each other,
In the
"Boat House"
~
The journal of your soul captures my heart
Like a lion out of its den
The memory of you, unfolds like a journal
Blowing in the wind
~
The softness of your skin, that of lambs wool
The fresh scent of your fragrance I cuddle,
Behind your ear
~
The kiss, the kiss we shared,
The sweetness of your softest spot
Your lips, comes from the deepest part of our
souls
~
A memory for the two of us, written down in a
journal
A journal of love, a journal, not to be forgotten
A journal of true love for others to read in the
future
To see how much we loved each other

Arthur Henn

Kissing You There

Warmth
~
That place between
Your ear and shoulder
The wind brushes your hair away
Kissing you there
No longer cold but a shiver
Runs up and down your spine
Feeling its ripples
Along every vertebrae
You close your eyes
A memory of passion
Overcomes you
~
Warming your beautiful
Soul

Life's Eternity

My heart grows fond of you
Every time I see you
The valleys have streams
So does my heart
~
When I close my eyes
Dreams of you become
Reality
~
Every breath you exhale
Becomes nourishment
For my soul
~
A heart beat away
Life's eternity
Comes my way
~
Life without you
Would not be
Paradise with you
~
Every footprint you make
A secret garden grows
~
Your smile
The highlights
Embracing your hair
~
Simulates
Gods beauty
In every way
~
Shaded colors
Highlighted
By crackling rays
Of light
~
Showing your true value
Of color

Emerging
Within every step
~
This days sunset
Comes to rest
Landscaping
A garden of colorful shadows
~
Embraced by
Gods
Painted sky

Light Shows Itself

Through the cracks of darkness
She hangs in the solitude
Of her own soul
~
Tainted
Polluted by her outside world
~
She waits
Bearing the beauty of her existence
Marked by a sign
Of
Forewarning
The color red
Signifies
Her
Hunger
~
Her desire to mate
She waits
Patiently
To fulfill her passion
Fulfilling her hunger
~
Digested
In the secrecy
Of darkness
~
Taken over by growth
Within her belly
Her mate
Metamorphoses
Into a chrysalis
Entwined by a web
Of what once
Was the home
Of darkness
~
The potency
To grow

Arthur Henn

Unfolding his
Spot on color
Shinny black
Onyx black
With the sharpness
Of red
Sharper than the edge of a razor
Traveling
Through the vain of his wings
Embracing his true nature
Like a sunrise
Unfolding onto
Darkness

Lines We Step Over

Stepping into the boundaries
Of another mans soul
The beast I see in this mans eyes
Is the reflection of my own soul
~
Words that should not have been spoken
Broken words unable to be put back together
~
Tears running down Gods cheeks
Only to show sadness
Of what he has created
~
What should be tears of joy
Is only pain in his heart
~
Like a painter
~
Proud of what he has created
Only to find years later
What was so bright in color
Has now faded
~
Still admired by those on the sidelines
But if they really understood
What was involved?
~
The moon would fall out of the sky
And the sunrise would last forever

Looking through the Lens of Life

I look through the lens of life
My soul bridges
The distance of what my eyes see
~
A photograph etched in my mind
My imagination
The power of words
Weaved for you to see
~
The essence of what the mind sees through the
lens
The essence of what the mind can do with what it
sees
The visible, is it what the mind really sees
~
Our hearts, the sacred ground of what the mind
sees
The expression of time landscaped by the bridge
of intimacy
The mirror image of eternity
A world seen through the passionate soul
My body is aware of the presence of death
Luminous by life, followed by death
The air that surrounds me is invisible
My thoughts
The air I breathe
Nature expresses the mysteries of God
The luminous presence
Of God
Is seen
Through the beauty of nature
That surrounds us
~
When you close your eyes, do we see the same
things the blind see?
When you open your eyes, do we see the same
things the blind see?
Do we hear what the blind hear?
Do we see what the blind hear?

~

The sensations of touch
Do we feel what the blind don't see?
Does the blind feel what we feel?

~

When I open my eyes I see light
Like the morning sunrise
Shining light into darkness
My mind sees natures beautiful colors

~

When I close my eyes I see darkness
My mind no longer sees natures beautiful colors
My soul captures the essence of beauty
A memory
A bridge of images captured by light
Etched in my mind

Love, Death, Guilt, and Sorrow

I'm here
Scrutinizing you
You're unable to see me
Gods' lustrous sunset
Reflects off
The sunglasses
You wear
~
I've watched you
Time and time
Again
~
The one you think of
Has been gone
For seven months now
You have been unfaithful
Every day of the month
Doing wrong
Having fun
~
Tears held back
You shed a tear
You are in love
With another man
One that never loved you
But took advantage of you
Emotions running wild
That night
You opened your soul
Out of desire
A one night stand
Now you're with child
~
The one you promised
Yourself to
Never showing up
It's late now
You're the only one
Waiting

Everyone waiting
Has gone home with someone
~
You start to worry
Thinking about the first time
You met
~
A love that's true
~
His last words
Whispered
In your ear
~
I'll be home soon
I love you
~
You pull into the driveway
Checking for mail
Like you have every day this year
~
This time a letter
Of condolence
An expression of sympathy
With another's grief
You weep
You cry
Tormented
By guilt
Your true love
Killed by friendly fire

Her Look Is Exquisite

Her beauty rests upon his piano
He plays Norah Jones music

He marvels what's on her mind
~
Black pearls
Gracefully embrace her neck
Black pearl earrings to match
Her black pearl eyes
Reflect that of chandelier lighting
Her hair shines like silk
His thoughts are to stop playing
Wanting to run his hands through
Her hair
~
Wine glass in her hand
Where is the one she thinks of?
The taste of fragrance in his wine
No comparison to her beauty
A beauty mark signature of
Her soul
Her heart unfolds to the songs he plays
She smiles
Saying thank you, goodnight

Her Secret Garden

The shoreline we walked
So many times before
Couples walk together hand in hand
Smelling the fragrance we smell
As the gentle sea breeze gracefully
Flows through your elegant hair
~
I trace your delicate contour
With the fingers of my mind
The softness of your skin is only
A memory left behind
What is it about you?
And your secret garden
That makes me want to love you
~
Your soul embraces mine
A memory I will never forget
The times we spent together
Were magical moments
Moments of love
Blooming
In your garden
~
Breaking away from the past
Finding my way home again
The love we had is gone
But you are not forgotten
~
Romance is a virtue the mind manifests
Time of the present is only a reflection
Of the past
The remembrance of your smile
Etched in my mind
As waves unfold along this shoreline
Footprints once there
Removed
Taken back out to sea
The beauty of your soul
Whispers in my ear

~

A seagull soars high above
Against Gods painted sky
That which reflects and shines
In your eyes

~

I stand here looking at you
This night's first star shines bright
Behind you
The still of the night moves along with you
She whispers
A dance we use to dance
Is still our dance
Another place
Another time
I will be here
Thinking of you
In your secret Garden

Holding On To My Heart

Somewhere in the valley of this distant mind of
mine
Echoes the joyous sound of a train whistle
That has blown so many times
~
This early morning cloud cover
Filtering the trickling light
Trying to burn its way through
The windowpane

~
Staring
In a trance
Mesmerized
By the soft falling rain
Flowing down
It's stained glass window
Echoing a remembrance
Not that far off
Not that long ago
~
Emotions flowing
Gracefully out of her tear soaked eyes
Holding her, not knowing why
~
She sleeps this night
Under the soft moonlight
~
Moonlit lines
Outline the silhouette
The contour of her beautiful form
~
A whirlwind of emotions
Settle in my mind
Whilst
My subconscious
Purses her form
~
Holding on to this heart of mine

It's homage to the emotions of her soul

~

My sense of touch
Encircles her heart
Our souls
Will find their home
Amidst the open sea

~

The unity
Of our spirit filled souls
Comfort each other's misfortune

~

Embraced by her love
Tears of joy
Her happiness
The rush of falling in love
The warmth of our courage
Thinking of each other
Wanting each other
Our souls are illuminated

~

This night's moonlit sky
Reflects a garden of red roses
Sealing the love
We have for each other

How I Met the One I Love

This soul of mine
Born out of darkness
Days turn into nights
Weeks turn into months
Months turn into years
No longer a boy
But a young man
Thinking he's a man
Unable to keep a girlfriend
Because I'm shy
My heart yearns
For love
~
When I'm not in school
I labor the halls with a vacuum
The first time I saw her I noticed
Her feet
The foot fetish thing, I admired in women.
A woman in heels
A woman in open toed wedged sandals
Yes it sounds silly
But this is what caught my eye
Turning around
Watching her walk down the hall
Like I have so many times before
Never seeing her face
Another voice echoing in my mind
"Watch where you are going"
This time I was immediately in love
Her walk, the way she would move
The way her hair bounced
Enticing me to want to get to know her
~
Still in High School
Afraid to ask her out
Scared she would say no!
I searched the halls for Barbara the one
That holds the key, key to the supply room
My heart stops I smile not knowing what to say

Excuse me can I have the key
Her smile from that moment on
Always turned my dark days blue
A plain Jane not a lot of makeup
She was beautiful enough
~
Afraid to ask her out
Scared she would say no!
~
Every time I would watch a love story
Every time I would see a man and woman kiss
Every time I would see a man and woman
holding hands
I would daydream it was her and I
~
I called work and ask the operator if I could talk
to
Barbara
I hear, her soft voice
"This is Barbara"
I'm the one that asked you for the key
Would you like to have some toast and tea?

I Cry

Sorrows amongst the winds of change
My spirit flies high as a dove
He smiles
Brighter than the sun
~
Why does one cry
Why am I sad
When I know his loving
Arms
Are wrapped around you
~
Shadows of your death
Creep up through
The cracks I walk on
~
Gods sedated sky
Puts darkness to rest
~
My soul rests with the evil
Broken clouds
Flow over
Above
This broken soul
~
Again
Drawn from the past
Lamenting
Grieving over the fallen
Longing for the present
What shall
Come to rest
Unfolds from the past
~
Emotions embraced
By the warmth of your loving arms
~
Laminated
By rays of your guided light
Falling through the cracks
Of the present

I look up into her sky

She knows not that I'm here
We are miles apart
There is a pond
I see her reflection in it, surrounded by fresh cut
grass
Embraced by her soft delicate ripples
Flowing to the other side
Where they dissolve, I do not know
~
I watch her soul dance
In this midsummer breeze
~
Her fragrance, that of her secret garden,
Wanders aimlessly my way
~
Her melodies flow all the way through this soul of
mine
~
Rose petals, rudderless, finding their way,
Dancing along with her soft melodies
~
Flowing my way
Holding on to her heart

I'm Here for You

When things go wrong
You are always there
The sacrifice of two hearts
Not that far apart
~
The sacrifice of letting go
Of the one you love
Closing in on my soul
For a love of friendship
You trust and love
~
It's no sacrifice on my part
Being here for you
We are two different worlds
When it comes to love
~
There you are
Here I am
Some things are better
The way they are
~
Letting go of him
Will be better
It's a sacrifice of love
That's rooted
In the bottom of your heart
~
It's no sacrifice that I'm here
To ease the pain you feel
Two hearts wanting to share
A love in a different way
Than you're use to

I'm So In Love With You

Lying here
With you
Amongst
Your secret garden
Growing old with you
Finding ways to stay young
~
The fragrance of your garden
Flows through the air
Forgetting who we are
Looking into each others eyes
~
Our eyes light up
Seeing each other smile
The loneliness we both once felt
Is gone
~
If we could just lie here
Looking into each others eyes
A little bit longer
We could watch the spring flowers grow
~
The beauty of it all
The colors in your eyes
Reflect that of spring flowers
Do you feel the same way I do?
~
Lying here next to me
The loneliness we share
Is now replaced with love
A love of two becoming one
The scent of your hair
The softness of your skin
The way we touch each other
Is a gift
Like the warmth of the sun
Flowing through your garden
~

Your beauty blankets the ground
These flowers grow from
I'm so in love with you

I'm Tough

On the surface
But not all the way through
~
Thinking of all the times my grandfather
Told me
I would be tough
All the way through
~
The way he would let the bottle
Scornfully take over
~
His best friend
Being
Life in the bottle
~
The iris of his eyes
Cold blue
~
They called him
Old
Blue eyes
~
A laugh and charm
I always liked
With an Irish accent
~
Feisty
And
Wicked
Always wanting to fight
Not always him
But the bottle
Living in him
~
Being his name sake
Wanting to be like him
I hear his Irish
Whisky
Voice

Reflections of My Soul

Telling me
Don't be like me
Make my name
A respectable name
~
You have a fine lady
Treat her right
Never being disrespectful
Like I have to your grandmother
~
This day I stand at your grave
My blood boils
Every one else's blood runs cold
The cold brushes against my cheek
Letting me know I'm still alive
~
Your immediate family
Sons and daughters
No tears or sorrows
That you are gone
~
The warmth of my soul
Pours out to you
Wishing you were still alive
Being your name sake
I Love You
Also missing you

~
I hear you knocking
On heavens
Door
~
Lord, take this badge away from me
Open up your kingdom's door
Let him embrace
Your loving warmth
More warmth, than he ever had
Before

Trials and Tribulations

I'm standing in the rain
Not knowing what to do
~
I look up into the star lit sky
Thinking of you,
Wondering why
~
Why do you keep letting him reel you in?
~
Life is a struggle, I know
We have to keep moving on
~
When I see you cry
Wanting you with wide open arms
My heart hurts wanting to love you
With this soul of mine

~
You are the fragrance of a rose garden
The nectar of honeysuckle
The brightness of color
That blankets these fields of wild flower
~
You always smile when you are in
My arms
We continue swaying with melodies
Lying in your heart
~
You close your eyes, thinking of him
While I'm holding you
~
You murmur his name
In delight
~
I know you miss him, wanting him to hold you
tight
Embracing you with the love I'm showing you
tonight

Reflections of My Soul

~

Holding you, being there for you
Is all you want?

~

Tears running down your cheeks
You whisper in my ear
Why can't you be him?
Just for a little while tonight

Arthur Henn

A Slice of Heaven

Will she remember me in these fields of daisies?
Reflections of each flower swaying in her eyes
Showing their true colors
Whites, yellows contrasted with green
Against her blue sky
~
Her smile
Bright, cheerful as the suns rays above
~
The times I kissed her face
Her beautiful face
~
What is it about your soul?
That strikes me so
~
Our walks in these fields
Fields of daisies
~
The love we shared with each other
The melodies our souls played together
With each sunrise
Sea breeze
Blanketing our sea of daisies
~
I will remember
The charm, the radiance, the warmth
We brought upon each others hearts
~
Your dress sways in the wind
Like the kite
We fly
High above
Against our clear blue sky
Tying a string to the old park bench
We lie next to
~
Our minds are overwhelmed by each others love
That we share
Passion unfolds

Reflections of My Soul

While we kiss each others lips
Tenderly biting down on your lower lip
Tasting the sweetness of your lips
Remembering the cotton candy we just shared
~
The scent of your perfume
Fragrance embracing your beautiful neck
~
I lower your shoulder straps
Securing the summer dress you wear
Exposing layered lace
Contouring your external beauty
~
Slowly
Running my fingers
Down
The opening
Of your
Soft smooth back
You shiver in delight
~
You my lady
You're a slice
Of heaven
~
Passion running through our souls
You're an angel in disguise
~
You breathe with softness
That of lamb's wool
Pulling each other closer
Our heads begin to spin
~
Our souls come to rest
Smelling the fragrance of your soul

Arthur Henn

Autumn Leaves Fall

Falling on me
Standing here
Thinking of you
~
Tired of being alone
Wishing you were here
Hearing your voice echo
Throughout the wind
~
My minds at ease
Thinking of the times
I fell in love with you
~
Time lingers on
Casting shadows amongst the leaves
Wiping away the tears
~
Tears
Falling upon these leaves
The winds of change
Serenades
Those that have fallen
Fallen amongst, others
~
Life has come
Now it has gone
Flowing in the midst of tears
Tears of
Autumn leaves

Beautiful As She Is

I walk the paths of life
Looking at her wonders
God in all his glory
Created a sphere of beauty
~
Beautiful as she is
She has a fire burning
Deep in the abyss of her hell
A gulf of streams separating her lake of fire
~
Fire separating good from evil
The tree of good and evil no longer exists
For Eve has eaten the last of its fruits
~
The beginning of man
Adam
Has diminished
What could have always been paradise?
Has now become an abyss of fire
No longer separated by its beauty
Field of streams

Arthur Henn

Beauty Is, The Eyes Of The Beholder

Bonded and stitched
To all four corners of the world
~
Cracks
Our sun seeps through
Inhibits warmth
For the immorality of your soul
~
Backlit colors
Excel through every rose
The ground you walk on
Shakes
With a tremor
Cultivating the earths
Core
~
What's been dormant to rupture?
Has reawaken
To reality
~
The ancient times
Has come to live
With
The present times
~
The dawn of iniquity
Does not unite
With the console of
Character
~
Beauty is amongst all living possessions
What is it the mind sees?
That captivates the human soul
~
If I went to heaven
Would you still be here?
~
Knowing what truth is
Were only a crown

Away

~

Beauty is, in the eyes of the beholder
The windows to our souls
~
Looking into your eyes
I see what truth is
Blanketing the sin of your soul
~
My thoughts, a reflection
Of
What's around me?
~
You heart
Is the key
To my
Soul

Desire

My hearts desire
Desire of ones beauty
Missing you
Wishing you were here
~
The stillness of night
Brings you closer to my
Soul
~
Your hearts
Sentimental value
Is the desire of wanting your
Soul
~
This night
Unfolds
With the beauty
Of your soul
~
The winds
Whisper
Your name in my ear
~
I see your smile
Embracing the wind
Hearing your soft voice
Whisper through the wind
~
The skies are dark
No moon in sight
The essence of your smile
Shines bright
~
Your beauty
Landscaped
With gracefulness
~
I've got a feeling
Deep inside

~

Feels like
I'm falling through the cracks of life
Blind faith
Leads me
To the love of your soul

~

Waiting for someone to love
The night shines
That of black Onyx

~

Life's doors
Close in on me
Stepping out into
The midsummer's breeze

~

Falling through the
Mist of summer
Winds blow through the canyons
Chasing the September moons
The dryness of September
Unfolds upon
Her
Autumn winds

~

The earth opens up
Swallowing
The emotions I feel for
You

~

Your love
Bleeds out on
Me

Melodies of Your Soul

Every time I hear rolling thunder
I see beauty in your eyes
The fire that burns in my heart
Dances in the iris of your
Blazing eyes
~
Reflections of crackling fire
Warmth braced upon our souls
Reflections of love
Swept away
~
Looking into your eyes
Consumed
By the
Warmth in your soul
A burning desire
In this heart of mine
~
Two hearts on fire
Burning with desire
We dance
Upon each others souls
~
The moment I saw you
From a distance
I looked upon you
Yearning
For a moment like this
~
You closed your eyes,
Tenderly I
Kiss your lips
Holding you
Loving you
Loving each other
It's a
Perfect autumn's night
~
Loving you

Reflections of My Soul

Throughout the early morning
Sunrise
Chasing the moon
Out of sight
Watching autumn's colors
Blanket her ground
Covering her so gently
~
Listening to your heart beat
Whispering sweet melodies
Upon the opening
Of my ear
~
Hearing the song
Of your soul

Arthur Henn

She Walks the Beach

Of every shore line
A footprint
Set in the sand
Only to be washed back out to sea
~
A seagull soars high above
In her clear blue skies
~
The roaring sound of waves
Rolls upon her shore
The cool sea breeze brushes up against her
cheeks
She feels the sun kiss her on the cheek
~
A yacht guided by her winds
~
She closes her eyes and dreams
Wishing the one she loves
Was there,
With her
Feeling his warm arms enclosed around her
Suddenly she turns around
He's not there
~
A footprint
Set in the sand
Only to be washed back out to sea

Summer Night's Angel

Summer night's storm
Just moved through
~
Light from street lamps reflect off her wet
pavement
Left behind from the storm
~
The one I think of, still smelling the fragrance of
her hair
A candle burns bright in her window tonight
Times I've walked by
Many times before
Wanting to stop, I knock on her door
Crazy in love with her
What can I do?
~
I'll never be the same after what she told me to
do
Her candle dances in the wind this night
I watch her looking out her window
Seeing if I'm there
~
Her eyes reflect candle light
Dancing in the night
I watch her eyes fill with tears of joy
You're the reason I'm here
Every night I walk by
You sit in front of the same window
Who are you waiting for?
~
This night you're in your white cotton dress
The one that makes me think
You're an angel
The way it forms, contours against your beautiful
figure
~
Wanting to see more of you
Surprised seeing you walk through the door

Arthur Henn

Looking into each others eyes
Brushing away
Tears of joy
With them wings of yours
Listening to my heart
Watching you
Falling in love with you
Like I have so many times before

Wild Roses

Running free
Running wild
With winds of change
Chasing darkness
Into this nights
Midnight moon
~
Her scent
Blossoming, Blooming,
Gracefully flowing in the breeze
Spreading her essence
Like rain
~
Her fragrance of summer
Lost
On the horizon of fall
Showing her beauty
Amongst his colorful autumn blanket
Of leaves
~
She stands tall
Swaying above the rest
Showing her beauty
Unfolding
Upon his setting sun
~
Fields and streams
Flowing strong
Nourishing her fields
Of wildflowers
Companionship
Embracing
Holding, hugging
The banks of
White Mountain

A Legacy

Built upon this mountain
I walk through its first snow fall
Whiter than white
Purer than angels breath
Undiluted
As clean mountain air
~
Who would ever know?
The purest of white
This first winter snow
Would be mixed
With death
Lying upon her snow
~
A full moon shines bright
Casting shadows
Upon
God's painted sky
~
White Mountain shakes
With anger
Gods' vale
Sheds tears
~
Mans innocence
Condemned
~
This valley
I look upon
Embraced by mountains
Having eyes
~
My darkest hour
Walking through
Bloodstained snow
Where shall I go?
Blood on my hands

Reflections of My Soul

~

Looking down
The eye
Of a buck
His antlers
Rise high into the clouds
The one she loves
Taken away from her

~

The sun rises far above the ground

~

Above me
The snow that covers
The ground I stand on
Melts away
Running into streams
Nourishing
Gods' valley
Showing the fragrance
Images of spring

~

Soiled blood
Engraves thyself
With the fruits
Of
Mother Nature

~

Spring turns into summer
Summer turns into fall
Falls autumn colors
Grace
Gods' valley
Mixed with shadows
Of his painted sky

~

What has come
Has passed

The memory still remains the same
Flowing with the winds of change
Ever so gently

Through out the autumn leaves

~

She stands on soiled ground
Missing the one she loves

~

Flowing clouds
Casting shadows
A new fur coat
Alone
Prepared
For her first winter storm

~

Snow, falling around her,
Blankets
What once was pure
Is now dark and soiled
With innocent blood

~

Driven by the purest of all storms
Once again
Covering the dead
Preparing the birth
Of
A new season
A legacy
For one to remember

Anna's First Kiss

I look over my shoulder
Into my shadow that follows me
A memory of one I loved
Puppy love that seemed so real to me
This day, does she still think of me?
~
My mind wonders back to that day
The day of our first kiss
Wondering, planning out that first date
How I was going to hold her
While giving her that first kiss
~
Here I am setting with her
My arm around her
Not caring about the movie
Playing on the big screen
The smell of her hair
The sparkle of lights reflecting in her eyes
My mind is jumping with joy that I'm setting
With her
Anticipation sets in wondering
If I should kiss her
~
She looks my way
Smiling
As if she wants to be kissed
~
I cradle her face
Only to kiss her cheek
~
Again she smiles
As she lies her head against my shoulder
Watching Gods painted sky come to rest
As this nights moon starts to rise
Thoughts of the times I watched her
Come out the door
~
Living across the street
Looking my way she would always smile

Asking me if I would like some ice tea
~
We were young
Too young to even know what a kiss was
Too young to know what love was?
A love that was bittersweet
~
My mind is bruised
From missing her
The groove we had on each other
The dance we use to dance
~
Tender years, they were
Laps of time, a laps of memory
You were once here
Now you are gone
There will be a day I will miss you
That day is today
(Now as I think of you!)
~
We never took time
To really know each other
Time ran out
As we drifted apart
Moving worlds apart
Never forgetting you
~
That first kiss
The kiss
Of
Anticipation
Wanting
To kiss your beautiful lips
Only to kiss you on your rosy cheek
Restless that night wondering
Why I didn't
Kiss you the way I wanted too
On our first date
~
A memory, shadows that follows me
Remembering our second date

Reflections of My Soul

Your smile shines as bright as your eyes
It all seemed to be on rewind
Watching the first time
I held you
Planning to kiss you
This time you say no
Pointing your finger to your lips
Looking up into my eyes
Telling me to kiss you
"Kiss me right here"
Right now
On these lips of mine
~

Thirty years have past
Never keeping in touch
Do you still remember?
Asking me to kiss, them lips of yours
A kiss that's bittersweet
Never forgetting that night
We held each other tight
Letting me kiss you there
~

You were that first love
Puppy love they say
I really never forgot
The love I never got over
It was bittersweet
~

Thirty years have past
I look forward to seeing you
At our high school reunion
Only to find you have died
My heart sunk when I saw
Your picture and read the news
Anna Ganote is no longer with us
~

Ann you are missed and I will never forget you!

Another Night

With out your love
I recovered
From my midnight blues
~
Lying down beside you
I feel you
Alongside me
Still warm
Looking into your eyes
~
Embracing
Your memories
Still fresh in my mind
~
Your heart is an open book
A treasure chest
Of love
Your fragrance
Flows through me
Like a sea breeze
~
Your hair is that
Of midnight
Shining bright
Among the falling stars
Unfolding upon its self
Around this nights full moon
~
Looking upon you
One has to be
In admiration
~
You're soft
You're clean
You glisten in its light
Embracing
Gods
Rising sun
~

Wait a minute
I can not go
Another night
Without loving you

Wanting You

Looking for the one I love
Her smile
Radiates, brighter than any falling star
Warming my soul
Not feeling cold anymore
~
Yearning for her love
Love I know nothing about
Deep down inside
My heart, closing in on me
Climbing this ladder from inside
Looking out
The windows of my soul
~
My eye sheds a tear
Releasing my emotions
Running down my cheek
Wondering
What am I to do?
~
Looking into your painted sky
Seeing you smile
You draw me in
With your setting sun
~
Your rainbow of colors
Embrace this soul of mine
Warming my heart
~
Looking upon the beauty
Landscaping my soul
Rose petals hanging onto my tears
Reflections of what I'm hanging onto
~
Wedged, open toed sandals
Ankle length dress

Reflections of My Soul

I'm so in love with you
No more sorrow
No more tears
Watching you come into my life
~
Twenty-nine years ago
When I kissed your lips
And said I do
Never thought I'd be this rough around the edges
This soon,
Realizing
The reality
Of really wanting you

"Love is the reason for our existence because we
were created out of love." -- Clary Lopez

Life comes upon us, from all directions
the first one to love us, notice us, is

Mom

In all her loving power
she smiles feeling movement within her womb.
~
The majestic gift, of a higher power,
two souls spending a magical night together
sharing the gifts of Love with each other.
~

God smiles, knowing the love of one being
created
Created out of Love

~

Clary, out of love you became a canvas of love
Created by love
Your "Mom" nourishing your soul,
To grow becoming the woman you are.
~
The opening and closing of this book is dedicated
to your "Mom"

Arthur Henn

Notes

Notes

Notes

Arthur Henn

www.ingramcontent.com/pod-product-compliance
Lightning Source LLC
LaVergne TN
LVHW011358080426
835511LV00005B/332